Cyber-Bullying is
Never Alright

Cyber-Bullying is Never Alright

ISBN 978-1468139402

Dedication

To all those who have suffered at the keystrokes of a cyber-bully. There is hope ... and there is help available. My prayer is that this book will motivate you to take action and find healing.

Foreword

Bullying in any shape or form is never alright and that's the message of this book. While most people are familiar with schoolyard bullying, cyber-bullying is a form of abuse that is not so well known. Although it shares some characteristics with traditional bullying, there are a number of elements that are unique to it. These include the use of devices such as cell phones, laptops and tablets as tools to torment and wound others. As the world becomes more and more connected through technology, the problem looks set to increase. Understanding the issues at hand is the first step to healing and this book will walk you through the process of identifying and dealing with cyber-bullying.

It is an intensely emotional experience to become a victim of a cyber-bully. It makes you question who you are, what you believe and how you behave. Your stomach lurches when you see the bully's name pop up on your phone or computer screen. You sit astounded at the venom and accusations directed your way. You wonder what friends and family would say if they knew what was going on.

I know because I've been there.

Debbie Roome 2012

Contents

Chapter One

Examples of Cyber-Bullying

Never be bullied into silence. Never allow yourself to be made a victim. Accept no one's definition of your life, but define yourself.

Harvey S. Firestone

Cyber-bullies have made headline news in many countries over the last few years. In some cases, the bullying has been so extreme that young people have taken their own lives. As technology advances and more and more people connect through cyberspace, the problem is ever increasing. Before taking an in-depth look at cyber-bullying, here are some true life cases and their outcomes.

May 2009: ABC News in Australia carried the followed story.

Two adolescent girls have been forced to leave one of Sydney's elite private schools because of cyber-bullying.

The girls were taken out of Ascham School after they published material on the social networking website, My Space, containing personal and possibly defamatory information about their classmates.

The comments included allegedly false statements about sexual behaviour, drug taking and alcohol consumption.

December 2009: The Daily Mail UK reported a rise in suicides by teenage victims of cyber-bullying. One such case was that of Megan Gillan, a pretty 15 year old schoolgirl who overdosed on painkillers earlier this year after spiteful messages were posted about her on the social networking site Bebo. The news story stated the following:

Like many parents, hers knew nothing of the perils of such sites, until Megan's death forced them to confront what had driven their daughter to take her own life.

'We had no idea the bullies were getting to her on the internet and on her mobile phone,' says Megan's father Mark, 53, a council civic attendant, from Macclesfield.

January 2010: ABC News.com reported that a 15 year old girl, Phoebe Prince had committed suicide after ongoing cyber-bullying by classmates in Massachusetts. She was an Irish immigrant who had been in the USA a short while.

Afterward, her fellow students came forward to tell school officials that Prince had been teased incessantly, taunted by text messages and harassed on social networking sites like Facebook.

February 2010: Stuff.co.nz in Christchurch, New Zealand carried the story of a Facebook hate campaign against the new principal of a high school with over 2000 pupils.

Warwick Maguire, who became Burnside High School's principal last November, has been targeted by a group called "I Hate Burnside's New Principal!!!" on social networking site Facebook."

Some of the group's 202 members have posted threatening and defamatory comments about Maguire and criticised changes he has made to the school, one of the country's largest.

September 2010: ABC News covered the story of 18 year old Tyler Clementi. After asking his roommate, Dharun Ruvi, for privacy for a few hours, Dharun set up a camera and taped a sexual encounter before streaming it live. Tyler committed suicide as a result of this.

A Rutgers University freshman posted a goodbye message on his Facebook page before jumping to his death after his roommate secretly filmed him during a "sexual encounter" in his dorm room and posted it live on the Internet.

January 2011: The Mail Online reported that two teenage girls had been arrested for creating a Facebook page for a classmate and posting inappropriate pictures on it.

Following an investigation the two girls have now been charged with aggravated stalking of a minor under 16.

According to Florida police, the Facebook page they set up featured an image of their victim's head atop a semi- naked child's body.

Another doctored photograph showed a man's genitals close to her body.

March 2011: The Mail Online told the story of callous teenagers who used Facebook to trick a UK schoolgirl into believing she had an online boyfriend. They then lied to her and said he had committed suicide and that she was the reason why. It was only after police checked records of sudden deaths and confirmed he had never existed that she learned the truth.

In a 'restorative justice meeting' with police, the girls responsible, accompanied by their parents, apologised to their victim.

Sergeant Paul Schofield, of Lancashire Police, said: 'When all is said and done this is online bullying.'

November 2011: The Press newspaper in Christchurch reported the following.

A teenage girl had to leave her school and move from the district after cell phone footage was taken of her performing a drunken sex act.' The Christchurch

4

District Court Judge Stephen Erber had the following to say. "The girl was humiliated because of rumour, gossip, and something called Facebook."

December 2011: Mail Online told the story of a military wife in the UK who was attacked on Facebook and Twitter because of her tattoos. These drew attention after her public appearances as part of the Military Wives' Choir.

She said: 'There were loads of nasty comments. It was hurtful. My tattoos made me stand out from the rest of the girls.

'Most people are lovely and supportive, but I've been really shocked by the reaction to my tattoos by people on the internet.'

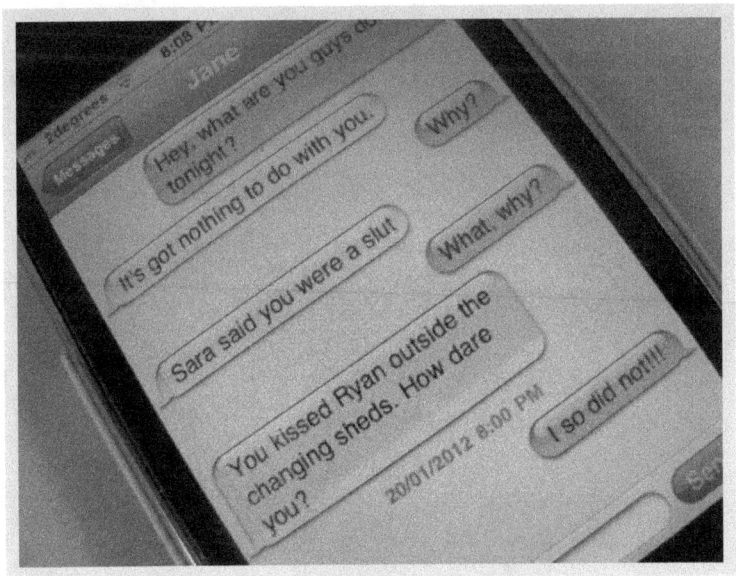

Chapter Two

Definition of Cyber-Bullying

Have the courage to say no. Have the courage to face
the truth. Do the right thing because it is right. These
are the magic keys to living your life with integrity.

W Clement Stone

*Marie wrote a weekly blog expressing opinions on
life and parenting. Happily married and mother to
three teenagers she shared some good stories and
most readers found her writing encouraging. Then an
acquaintance named Shelly took offence to an article
about piercings and tattoos. It started with a nasty
comment on the blog that Marie deleted. Shelly was
angered by this and sent her a message asking what
had happened to freedom of speech. Marie responded
and tried to explain what she meant by the article.
Within a month, the problem had spiralled out of
control and Shelly was bombarding Marie with
comments on her blog, insults on Facebook, and texts
that warned her to stop writing rubbish.
Overwhelmed and guilt-ridden, Marie decided it
wasn't worth the pain and gave up her blog. Even
then, Shelly wouldn't leave her alone and Marie
withdrew into herself and eventually ended up
depressed and suffering from low self esteem.*

Before looking at the definition of cyber-bullying, it
can be useful to understand the more traditional
forms of bullying. In all cases, bullying can be

defined as the repeated and systematic harassment and attacks on other people. It can be inflicted by individuals or groups of all ages and both sexes and can occur anywhere. Typical behaviours associated with bullying include the following:

- harm is intended
- repetitive attacks
- physical violence
- verbal abuse
- teasing
- name calling
- threats and intimidation
- negative references to gender and race
- theft of money and possessions
- exclusion from peer groups
- imbalance of power
- organised and systematic attacks
- controlling behaviour
- emotional hurt

What Bullying is Not
There are certain actions that cannot be classed as bullying unless the tone and intensity suddenly changes for the worse:

- playful teasing
- a one-off fight
- rough and tumble or play fighting that are not meant to harm or upset

All About Cyber-Bullying

Cyber-bullying is a relatively new form of bullying that has evolved with the development of information technology and as more of us become connected in cyberspace, the problem is growing at a rapid rate. Because it is perpetrated online or through cell phones and other devices, it does not generally include physical violence or theft. However, it does encompass the other elements of bullying mentioned above. Bill Belsey, a Canadian educator defines cyber-bullying as follows. "Cyber-bullying involves the use of information and communication technologies to support deliberate, repeated, and hostile behaviour by an individual or group, that is intended to harm others."

Technology has shrunk the world so that we can communicate instantly at the touch of a button – and this is not just for the rich. The majority of people living in a first world country have access to a cellphone, computer and other modern technology – and so do many of those living in third world countries.

In many senses these connections are wonderful things. They enable us to keep in touch with family and friends and communicate about our plans and movements. We send messages and photos thousands of miles across the world at the tap of a button. Childhood friends can be traced, we keep in touch with family across the world and new friendships can develop, but like all things in life, there is a downside. There are those among us who turn these forms of technology into a negative by cyber-bullying others.

Like schoolyard bullying, cyber-bullying exists on a spectrum that ranges from mild to severe. All levels are abusive and you should never suffer in silence if targeted. In some cases, the perpetrator is known to the victim, and in others their identity is a mystery. When social networking sites such as Facebook, Bebo and Myspace are used, the parties involved normally know each other. However, it is not uncommon for perpetrators to hide behind user names or create fake identities and profiles.

As technology advances and it becomes cheaper to connect, more of us - across all age groups - are finding cyber-bullying a problem. Here are some of the ways we link to others through cyberspace:

- laptops
- desktop computers
- tablets
- cell phones
- Xbox, PlayStations and other gaming consoles

The above devices can be used to access the following forms of communication:

- social networking sites such as Facebook, MySpace, Bebo, YouTube and Twitter
- online forums and chat rooms
- emails
- instant messaging

- text messages
- comments on blogs, websites and other online material

The type of content posted varies greatly but all of it has the power to harm you. Some cyber-bullies have a preferred method of attack while others use an array of weapons. While some content is only viewable by the person receiving it, other messages, video footage and photos are posted in public places with the potential of going viral. This means it can be shared and passed on and has the potential of being seen by literally millions of people. The rapidity with which this type of content can be shared makes it difficult to remove completely from the online world. Some common forms of cyber-bullying include the following:

- gaining a person's confidence and getting them to reveal personal or sensitive information that they then use against them
- posting photos or videos that show the victim in an embarrassing situation or state of undress
- pasting victim's faces onto nude photos or similar and sharing these on social networking sites
- Tweeting false accusations
- commenting negatively and vindictively on blog posts and online articles
- emailing messages with insults or attacks against the person's character or appearance
- nasty comments and threats in chat rooms

- posting personal details such as the victim's contact details and email addresses
- encouraging others to join the attack against the person
- setting up fake identities on Facebook and similar sites and using these to torment their victim
- inflammatory messages that spread gossip and lies
- publicly excluding the person from social activities and groups
- text messages that hurt, threaten or humiliate
- cyber-bullying can be an extension of schoolyard or physical bullying

When the cyber-bully is known to you, you will probably go to great lengths to avoid face-to-face contact at school or work. You may also harbour a fear that the online abuse will escalate to a greater level if you behave in a manner that provokes the bully. If the cyber-bully is anonymous, there will be the added problem of fear and virtually everyone you know becomes a suspect.

The scale of cyber-bullying can vary from sporadic emails and texts to daily attacks that are persistent, consistent and invasive. Several mediums may be used at any given time. In some cases, cyber-bullying progresses to cyber-stalking where the level of attack increases and violent threats are made.

As children have started using the internet and cell phones at younger ages, the problem of cyber-bullying has been reported in those as young as six and seven. On the other end of the scale, older people are also finding cyber-abuse a problem. This can manifest in the workplace or at home and is usually unexpected and extremely damaging emotionally.

Cyber-bullying and Cyber-Stalking

Cyber-stalking is a step beyond cyber-bullying and you should seek professional help immediately if this happens to you. It may begin as cyber-bullying and then degenerate into stalking. Signs of this form of abuse are as follows:

- The stalker may be an ex-partner or someone you dated. They can't accept the relationship is over and hound you via the internet.
- People in public positions of service may attract stalkers who disagree with their policies.
- Many stalkers have mental problems and create a fantasy relationship with you in their minds.
- The stalker may reveal information that proves they are watching your movements both physically and online.
- They sign up to social networks and chat rooms with the sole purpose of communicating with you.
- Violent threats are common.
- They try and force you to change your behaviour by threatening you.

There is a fine line between cyber-bullying and cyber-stalking but if you feel threatened in any way, report the abuse to the police immediately and persist until they do something to help you.

Chapter Three

A Closer Look at Cyber-Bullies

When a bully taunts his/her target, there is no playfulness in the attack, no matter how much the bully may protest, 'I was just teasing'!

Barbara Coloroso

Marc was given a cell phone for his eighth birthday and soon collected all his friends' numbers. The boys had fun with their phones and learned to use all the available features. One of these friends snapped a picture of Marc when he was changing for physical education at school. Small in stature, with thin arms and legs, Marc was devastated when he realised the photo had been passed on to all his friends, some of whom forwarded it to other people from school. By that evening, the picture had made its way onto Facebook accompanied by a number of negative comments. Marc spent the night crying into his pillow until his distraught parents got the truth out of him. They went to the school the next day and as a result the principal spoke to the culprits, explaining what pain their actions had caused Marc. The picture had spread so far by that time that it was impossible to completely remove it from the internet. Marc suffered emotionally for months as he agonised over what had happened.

Cyber-bullies are often referred to as trolls. Most people will have heard the tale of the Three Billy

Goats Gruff. The goats want to cross the stream to the lush meadow on the other side but one by one, they are confronted by an ugly, mean troll that lives under the bridge. The troll had previously eaten every creature that dared walk on the bridge but the goats outwitted him and he was never heard of again.

In modern day society, the word troll has an additional meaning that is just as nasty as the creature that lived under the bridge. The Online Oxford Dictionary defines troll as follows:

- (in folklore) an ugly cave-dwelling creature depicted as either a giant or a dwarf.
- *informal* a provocative email or posting intended to incite an angry response.
- *informal* a person who sends such an email or submits such a posting.

When cyber-bullying starts up, you will almost certainly be caught by surprise. It's as though an ugly troll has jumped out in front of you and it's not a pleasant experience. At the same time, you will experience a wide range of feelings that may fluctuate from one day to the next. Hurt, bewilderment, humiliation and fear are common and you may also feel extremely angry. Thoughts of revenge and violence are not uncommon but should never be acted upon.

Each cyber-bullying situation is unique but there are some broad categories of trolls that can help you recognise the type of abuse that is being inflicted. The groupings are broad and by no means comprehensive but can help you evaluate what you are dealing with.

Nitpickers take great delight in picking apart your work, updates, comments and writing. Grammar, punctuation, spelling, website content and messages are pulled apart and the bully wears you down by their persistence. The endless criticism often leaves you bewildered and demoralised to the point where you give up.

Verbal cyber-bullies are masters of words and turn them against you with great effect. They typically use sarcasm, derision and demeaning language and may start false rumours that they spread across social networking sites. Their choice of words is designed to dominate and humiliate and the emotional scars from their accusations can be deep and painful. Racial attacks often fall into this bracket.

Cyber-bullies with long memories hold something against you that may have happened years ago. It could be an unresolved argument, a mistake in business or a teenage fight, but they regularly drag it up. Comments about your supposedly inappropriate behaviour a decade ago may be plastered all over Facebook or you may receive venomous emails telling you why you don't deserve to be happy in life.

Familiar cyber-bullies know you well. They have made it their business to find out your email address, cell number, Facebook page, Twitter handle, and they often go as far as tracking down your home address and land line number as well. Some have intimate knowledge such as where birthmarks are, what your favourite foods and drinks are and what bad things you may have done in the past – and they're not shy to spread these facts across the internet.

Persistent cyber-bullies are convinced that they are right and you are wrong. They use every opportunity to point this out online and if you engage with them, they will go into great detail about your inadequacies and how you have posted incorrect information. They may go through everything you put online and tear it apart. Some go as far as creating non-existent friends who supposedly back up their claims about your ineptness.

Expert cyber-bullies claim to be more qualified than you and feel they are in a position to negate your work and worth in a particular field of expertise. This may be in the workplace or in connection with writing that you have online. The reality of this situation is that the troll is often a wannabe. Even if they have the education or knowledge, they are probably not using it effectively. It's more likely, however, that they're unemployed and uneducated and have nothing better to do than annoy you.

Cyber-bullies with clones create different user names and bombard you with abusive messages in an effort to make you believe that a group of people are against you.

Sexual cyber-bullies make sexual threats and innuendos and can be frightening, especially to a young teenage girl. Sexting is the practice of sending texts with sexual content, whether it be written or photographic.

Serial cyber-bullies engage in online bullying as a part of life. They may torment several victims at the same time or move from one to another. They lurk around online forums and chat rooms and launch their attack when they see something they don't like or don't agree with. These types of cyber-bullies are often strangers to their victims and thrive on stirring up trouble.

Narcissistic cyber-bullies are self-centered and cannot empathise with others. They make themselves feel good by putting you down and seem unaware of the consequences of their actions. On the surface they may appear confident and self-assured but in reality they are insecure and self absorbed.

Impulsive cyber-bullies may have anger management problems and write and post without thinking. Their attack against you is often random and varied and made in the heat of the moment.

Client cyber-bullies attack those that serve them. This is seen in situations where an employee is bullied by those they serve. People with occupations such as teaching and nursing often fall into this category. The abuse is seen when pupils attack their educators online or patients criticise and belittle nursing staff through emails and texts.

Secondary Cyber-bullies generally pop up when the primary perpetrator is known to you. A school acquaintance may stir up an online attack against a person and encourage others to join in. Some secondary trolls do so to save face and avoid being cyber-bullied themselves.

Corporate cyber-bullies are often in a position of authority and make life unpleasant for you as an employee. They do this by tormenting you through scathing memos and emails. Noncompliance to demands to work extra hours or act in an unethical manner can lead to an increase in this type of bullying.

It is important to remember that you cannot reason with cyber-bullies. They are experts at sidestepping issues, deflecting blame and answering questions with accusations. They relish the anonymity of bullying online and even if they are known to you, they normally feel free to write things that they would hesitate to say face to face. This means that the attack can be extremely cutting. Their message may also be confusing as written communication can be difficult to interpret without the aid of body language, facial expression, voice tone, and eye contact.

Third Parties in Cyber-bullying

Online bullies often have an audience, especially if they post messages on social networking sites where information is shared among friends and passed on for others to read. There are three possible responses from onlookers:

- They ignore the situation as they don't want to get involved. Even if they recognise the posts as abusive, they choose to say and do nothing.
- They side with the bully and add comments of their own to back them up. This is called secondary bullying and in some cases, the primary bully may have several secondary bullies aiding them in their attack.
- They side with the victim. It is possible that they open themselves up as a target by doing this but some friends are willing to pay the price. If this does happen, the victim may feel guilty that their friend is now suffering because of them.

More about how Cyber-Bullies Operate

A cyber-bully generally has preferred means of communication and will focus on these when attacking you. In the case of an anonymous bully, they may use a bunch of different email addresses in an effort to avoid being identified. Email messages are often longer and more explicit than Facebook updates or text messages.

Online Forums and chat rooms are often home to lurkers who home in on anyone they think is vulnerable. The remarks they drop into discussions and conversations are often incendiary, critical and negative and are designed to provoke a reaction. This type of bully may not have anything against you personally. They just get a kick out of stirring things up and pick on anyone who they think would make a good victim.

Facebook and other social networking sites are commonly used by people who are 'friends' with each other. Some of these friends may be mere acquaintances or friends of friends that you have never met. One of these people may start bullying by making a comment on something they don't agree with. This is presented as a friendly criticism, a concern, or an objective view point. When the commenting continues or degenerates into nastiness, the line has been crossed and the communication becomes cyber-bullying.

How Cyber-Bullies Respond if Confronted

Bullies normally respond to confrontation in a predictable manner. Many victims of cyber-abuse have tried communicating with their attacker but find it a futile exercise. When a cyber-bully is confronted or questioned about their behaviour they typically respond in one or more of the following ways:

- Denial – the cyber-bully will turn the blame back onto their victim with accusations that they are blowing things out of proportion. They may say the matter is trivial or in the past and that the person needs to move on. Blaming the victim for the problem is part of denying their own responsibility in the situation.
- Retaliation – the cyber-bully sidesteps the issues raised by the victim and launches a further attack against them. This attack often includes lies and accusations and detracts from the original problem. A confrontation, face-to-face or online, can lead to a greater intensity in

cyber-bullying and should be handled carefully and thoughtfully.

- Victimhood – the cyber-bully turns the situation around and blames their victim for causing them upset and distress. Manipulation is common in this scenario and emotions may run high. Cyber-bullies often present themselves as the victim and say they are offended and hurt by the other person's response and accusations. They may bring health issues and stress into play at this stage and avoid answering the original question raised.

In most cases it is best to completely ignore a cyber-bully while silently gathering evidence. When it is time to confront them, this should be done by someone with authority and experience in this kind of situation.

Cyber-bullies can be compared to a dog with a filthy old bone that they can't leave alone. Their attack against you is generally ongoing, relentless and focused and can be extremely damaging emotionally.

Chapter Four

What Motivates Cyber-Bullies

Bullying slowly erodes the soul of the victims and does destroy their sense of self-worth and self-esteem.

Katie Mann

Jonathan worked for a large retail group and was promoted to store manager at a young age because of his qualifications, natural ability and positive attitude. Sandy was passed over for the position as she had a tendency to gossip and show favouritism. She started emailing and texting Jonathan and made his life miserable. Complaints included the distribution of work, his communication skills and lack of dress sense. Jonathan chose to ignore her and this angered her to the point where she started spreading rumours by emailing the top management of the company. She did this by posing as customers and used several email addresses that she set up especially. The CEO was aware of Sandy's issues with Jonathan and hired an IT expert to track the source of the emails. Sandy was fired and Jonathan retained his position. Even so, the stories circulated for several months and he eventually resigned and moved away to make a fresh start.

People bully for a number of reasons – but none of them make bullying alright. Understanding what motivates your cyber-bully can give you some insight into their behaviour and also a sense of the best way to handle the situation.

- Many cyber-bullies enjoy the sense of power they have over their victims. The response they get often encourages them to continue and even intensify their attacks.
- Some people bully online to try and increase their own popularity or sense of worth. It may increase their self esteem in a strange way and they enjoy presenting themselves as an expert.
- Jealousy is another reason people bully.
- Bullies may torment others in a bid to get attention or to cause fear in their victim.
- Cultural and racial differences can cause cyber-bullying and in these cases, hurtful comments and discrimination are common.
- People who have been brought up in dysfunctional families or who have experienced social rejection themselves are more likely to bully others.
- In some cases, bullies are victims of bullying themselves and lash out at you to try and make themselves feel better.
- Personality disorders can make it impossible for a person to see that their bullying is inappropriate.
- Mental problems are another cause of cyber-bullying.
- Immaturity is a factor in some cases of cyber-bullying. The perpetrator may be unaware of the level of pain and emotional suffering they are inflicting on their victim. This is

sometimes the case with children and teenagers.

- Some people cyber-bully anonymously with the mistaken belief that they will never be caught.

Who do Bullies Target

Some groups of people are targeted more frequently than others but this does not mean it is acceptable in any way. Bullying is always inappropriate and the victim should never, ever be blamed for bringing it upon themselves. They have enough to deal with without being accused of causing the problem as well. The following are some typical bullying scenarios but it should be remembered that people who appear 'normal' and don't fit into any of these groups are still targeted:

- children and adults with mental and physical disabilities
- people with different colour skin and appearance to local residents
- people with different cultural and religious beliefs
- teenagers and children who are considered nerds, geeks and losers
- people with annoying habits or characteristics
- people who don't dress fashionably or behave in a socially acceptable manner
- those who come from a poor socioeconomic bracket
- people who deliberately provoke others by acting in a contrary or inappropriate manner

- anyone who stands out as being different
- sometimes the victim is someone who just happens to be in the wrong place at the wrong time

Control is Part of Bullying

Cyber-bullying is a form of exercising control over another person. They may want to make you behave in the way that they perceive as right and they expend a lot of time and energy in pursuing this goal. Their aim is for you to live life by their rules and they can't seem to understand that you are entitled to your own point of view. In some cases people cave in and try and follow a bully's demands. In the case of an online bully this may include removing web content, changing the way they write and communicate or updating the way they dress. Here are some ways in which control plays out in cyber-bullying:

- A controller attacks the mind and emotions and tries to force you to think in a certain way.
- A controller will contradict you as though they know more about you than you do yourself. This is communicated by statements that assume intimate knowledge of what you are thinking.
- A controlling bully will try and define you and force you to see yourself in the same way they do.
- A controller may promise to back off if you comply with their demands. Don't ever agree to this. It will only make matters worse.

- A controlling cyber-bully will often target a person's gifts and abilities and try and diminish these.

It is important to recognise the control factor and know that the perpetrator is irrational. They cannot be reasoned with and will usually defend themselves to the end. This can cause arguments to spiral out of control and cyber-abuse to multiply.

When the time comes to confront a controlling cyber-bully, it is essential to focus on their behaviour. If you focus on their arguments and specific content of the cyber-abuse, they will tie you up in verbal knots. You need to address the fact that their behaviour patterns are wrong and inappropriate and will no longer be tolerated.

Chapter Five

Signs & Effects of Cyber-Bullying

The best indicator of a sociopathic serial bully is not a clinical diagnosis but the trail of devastation and destruction of lives and livelihoods surrounding this individual throughout their life.

Tim Fields

Maxine taught 11 and 12 year old children at a public school. She had strict rules in the classroom and some of the pupils rebelled against this. They started a Facebook page called 'The Worst Teacher' and posted photos and video clips taken on their cell phones during class. Comments were made under a fake profile name that all the children had access to. Maxine first heard of this through an anonymous note on her desk. She was devastated when she found the Facebook page and saw the content and criticisms. The principal of the school supported her through this time and advised her to save each page of the 'Worst Teacher Profile' as evidence. They then contacted Facebook to advise them of the abuse and the profile was deleted. Maxine was reluctant to return to teaching the class but the principal said she needed to show the youngsters that they had not won the battle. A bullying expert was called in and took the class through a six week course on the effects of all types of bullying, At the end of it some of the pupils wrote an apology note to Maxine, saying they hadn't realised how damaging their actions had been.

Cyber-bullying is first and foremost an emotional attack and you may be shocked by the feelings it stirs in you. The hurt, fear, anger and frustration may be so great that thoughts of violence, murder and revenge pass through your mind. Some people vent their pain by smashing things while others bottle it up, only to have a complete emotional meltdown further down the track. While the impact is often greater on a vulnerable child or teen, adults also suffer tremendous emotional pain when targeted by an online bully. The above reactions are not unusual and to deal with them, you need to acknowledge the depth of pain that cyber-bullying has caused you.

Part of the process of dealing with the hurt is telling partners, parents, siblings and friends what is going on in your personal life. You don't need to tell everyone – just a few people you trust. Many victims are ashamed to speak about what they are suffering as they feel they are somehow to blame. Don't hide your pain as it will ultimately make the situation worse.

Here are some of the common signs that indicate someone is being cyber-bullied. It may be useful to show this list to a trusted friend or family member when telling them about the abuse you are suffering.

- A change in habits when it comes to cell phone and computer usage. This may escalate to obsessional checking of emails and text messages, or the person may choose to totally isolate themselves from technology. The victim avoids certain activities and may cut back on internet time and using their cell phone for fear of further harassment. A change either way can be an indication of cyber-bullying.

- Secretive behaviour when using the computer. This includes turning the screen off or minimising a window when someone walks past. The person may appear nervous and jumpy while using technology.
- Social withdrawal and isolation is common, especially if the identity of the cyber-bully is known and they mix in the same social circles as the victim.
- In younger children, bed-wetting may occur.
- Nightmares and broken sleep can be caused by cyber-bullying.
- Angry outbursts at family members may be an expression of the emotion the person is struggling with. Try and see past this to what really caused it.
- Sadness and depression are common, especially when the cyber-bullying is being kept a secret.
- Poor concentration and acting out of character can be a sign that a teen or child is being cyber-bullied.
- A teenager may be reluctant to confide in a parent for fear of losing their cell phone and computer privileges.
- In certain circumstances, cyber-bullying can lead to financial losses and cutting of hours at the person's work place.

- Fear of intimidation and fear of possible retaliation can prevent a person of any age from reporting cyber-abuse.
- The person may suffer from lowered self esteem and feel disempowered, useless, ugly and incompetent.
- A loss of interest in activities previously enjoyed.
- Some victims of cyber-bullying suffer from intense fear, especially if the identity of the bully is unknown.
- Shame is a sign that a person is being bullied. They are embarrassed that someone would target them in this way and may feel that in some way they deserve it.
- Hurt is inevitable when a person is being cyber-bullied. Whether the perpetrator is known to them or not, it is an emotionally painful experience to be victimised in such a way.
- Anxiety is a common effect and the person may be on edge and nervous, especially when reading text messages or emails.
- Cyber-bullies can disempower you if you allow them to make you change your behaviour in order to slow or reduce the abuse.
- Thoughts of suicide or suicidal actions can be the result of prolonged cyber-bullying.

Signs that a Person may be Suicidal
In extreme circumstances, cyber-bullying has the potential to cause a person to want to die. This is not normally an overnight decision but one that is made

after extended periods of torment. If you recognise any of the following signs in yourself, or if a family member or friend of a cyber-bullying victim sees the signs in their loved one, it is essential to seek help immediately:

- excessive moodiness and crying spells
- change in routines including sleeping and eating patterns
- social withdrawal
- increased use of alcohol or drugs
- feeling trapped and like there's no hope of escape
- engaging in risky behaviour such as driving recklessly as though they have a death wish
- giving away valued items and setting personal affairs in order
- preoccupation with death and violence
- showing interest in, or researching ways to die
- making a big deal of saying goodbye to friends
- making statements about wanting to die and feeling worthless

Cyber-Bullying and Mutual Friends

In some cases, the cyber-bully may be friends with some of your friends. This places them into what some would consider an awkward position. They know both of you and possibly have heard both sides of the story. They may even agree with you and privately condemn the cyber-bully's behaviour ... but that's where it ends. They will probably explain their feelings and actions in one or more of the following ways:

- I want to remain neutral as you're both my friends and I'd like to keep it that way.
- It's not my place to say anything. The issues are between you two and have nothing to do with me.
- I don't want to get involved as the bully may turn against me as well and start sending me abusive emails and messages.
- It's not my quarrel and I may complicate matters if I get involved.

These types of reaction can be demoralising and devastating. The best thing you can do is try and see the situation from their point of view and forgive them for their lack of support. Then look for those friends who have the courage to come alongside you, hold your hand, and say 'we're in this together'.

A Word to Friends of Cyber-Bullied People
Cyber-bullying is not a mild disagreement, a childish tiff or something anyone deserves. It is a terrible experience that leaves victims demoralised, fearful, and with low self esteem. People who witness what is going on need to say something if they disagree with the abuse. Silent support is generally not helpful as when the attacks come, the victim feels isolated and afraid. Cyber-bullies need to be confronted by those who witness their abuse. This does not mean bullying them back but simply stating that their behaviour, and the tone and content of their messages is inappropriate.

Encouraging a friend to seek help is also an important responsibility for those who care about them. In some cases, it can be good to mention the problem to someone in authority. This is especially so when young people are involved. A word with a teacher, school principal or parent can be a step towards stopping the bullying.

Abuse in any form is never alright and getting involved when a friend is being cyber-bullied is usually the right thing to do.

Subject: Hello

Headers: Show All Headers

We all hate u!!!

Delete | Reply | Forward | Redirect

Mark as: ▼ Move | Copy

Chapter Six

Where does Cyber-Bullying Take Place

When we are afraid we ought not to occupy ourselves with endeavouring to prove that there is no danger, but in strengthening ourselves to go on in spite of the danger.

Mark Rutherford

Jonah was a journalist who branched out and wrote a mystery novel. This was published by a small niche company and Jonah was responsible for most of the marketing. He used Twitter, Facebook, and other social networking sites to spread the word and on the way, picked up a cyber-bully. He had no idea who the person was but guessed it was a woman who was using several fake ID's. She had obviously read his book and subsequently posted criticism in several places and gave him a bad review on Amazon.com. She picked the plot apart, tore into his grammar and scorned his style. He was in the difficult position of trying to get his name out to the public while fighting off the attacks from the cyber-bully. He had some success with blocking the bully's email addresses but she created new ones that slipped through the cyber-barriers he put in place. The police were unhelpful and after a local newspaper printed a negative review based on the bully's comments, he considered quitting. A breakthrough came when the publisher remembered a writer who had submitted a novel that was substandard and had been rejected. In response, she had bombarded their office with abusive emails and phone calls. The police took notice when approached again and it turned out the same woman was behind the cyber-abuse. She was angry that Jonah's book had been published and hers hadn't. He was simply in the wrong place at the wrong time but this did not minimise the rejection and pain this woman caused him.

Cyber-bullying takes place in the office, at school, in the library, at the mall, and anywhere that traditional bullying takes place. However, there is one big difference. The bully does not have to be physically present. They can reach you anywhere that you access your emails or use your cell phone. Here then are some of the places where you may find yourself vulnerable:

At Home
Cyber-bullying can reach a victim at home and this is one of the major differences between cyber-bullying and schoolyard bullying. In normal circumstances, home is a safe place where victims of schoolyard bullying are generally assured of peaceful nights and weekends.

Conversely, cyber-bullying is invasive and breaks physical boundaries as it reaches the victim electronically. Instead of feeling safe at home, you may suffer the greatest attack there as you read your emails, text friends and surf the net. You may be reluctant to do all of the above for fear of the next message from the bully. Cyber-bullying violates the safety and sanctity of home and the intense emotional pain caused by this should not be underestimated.

At Work
Some cyber-bullies focus on tormenting you at work. They may be a co-worker or someone who is jealous of your career. The abuse can come through as texts or emails or they may place derogatory comments on your online work.

A manager who is a cyber-bully can make life very difficult for you and may pass the abuse off as necessary correction and training. Memos that mention you and your apparent mistakes as an example to all and sundry are one way they may do this and get away with it.

At School
Teens are the largest age group to engage in cyber-bullying and school is where much of the action takes place. The abuse may take the form of a constant stream of cyber insults. Texts, remarks on Facebook and emails can all be passed on through cell phones and other devices and can be done subtly without anyone in authority noticing. When teenagers gang up to bully a person, they can make their life a misery by the sheer volume of communication generated.

In Public Areas such as Malls and Libraries
Wherever you can connect to cellular networks or the internet, a cyber-bully can access you too. People are in touch wherever they go these days and whether you are having coffee at the mall with a friend,

studying for a chemistry exam at the library, or riding a horse in the country, a cyber-bully can reach you.

On Holiday or out of the Country
Cyber-bullying can reach literally right around the world. If you travel to another country for a few weeks you will still be connected to home in some way. Most people take their cell phones with them and roaming is available in many countries. Your email addresses won't change and if you use Facebook or similar, it is unaffected by your physical location.

The invasive nature of cyber-bullying makes it very hard to deal with. You may feel overwhelmed and that there is no escape from your tormentor – even if you travel to the other side of the world. That is not true. Cyber-bullying is never alright and there *are* ways you can get through this difficult time in your life.

Chapter Seven

Help for Teens and their Parents

It takes more courage to reveal insecurities than to hide them, more strength to relate to people than to dominate them, more 'manhood' to abide by thought-out principles rather than blind reflex. Toughness is in the soul and spirit, not in muscles and an immature mind.

Alex Karras

Charles and Sarah were at their wits end with their daughter. Donna was 15 and over the last few months had changed from a carefree teenager into an introverted grump. All questions were met with attitude and her parents despaired, wondering where their friendly, vivacious child had gone. The breakthrough came when Donna saw a news item on television about a cyber-bullied teen who had taken her own life. She fled to her room in tears, leaving her bemused father staring after her. After discussing it with his wife, they wondered if Donna was a victim of cyber-bullying. They sat her down and finally got to the truth behind the upset. A group of teens at school had been victimising her because she was academically bright, and because she wore thick glasses. Donna sobbed as she showed them cruel texts and digitally altered pictures on Facebook that showed her with saucer-like spectacles.

Her parents were appalled and her father started making plans to remove Donna's laptop from her bedroom and limit her cell phone usage. To his surprise, this provoked an even greater reaction from his daughter. She shouted and screamed, accusing her parents of 'totally wanting to ruin my life'. As she ran from the room, she yelled over her shoulder, "This is exactly why I didn't tell you!"

Teenage years are centred round social interaction and they are constantly in touch, communicating by texting, emailing and chatting online. Because of this and their relative immaturity, they are the age group most vulnerable to cyber-bullying. It is overwhelming for a young person to find themselves suddenly bombarded with volumes of cyber-abuse and most have little idea of how to handle the problem. Generally speaking, they keep their pain to themselves or share it only with close, trusted friends. Parents normally have no clue as to what is transpiring and may be bewildered by the changes in their offspring. It is essential that teenagers don't try to handle cyber-bullying on their own. They need to communicate with their parents about what is going on although this can be difficult to do. Here are some things that teens and parents need to be aware of when working through the pain of cyber-bullying.

Dos and Don'ts for Teenagers
This is not an exhaustive list and not everything will apply to you. Read it through and take what you can from it ... and remember that your parents love you and only want the best for you. Open communication is the best way for all of you to get through this time in your life.

Do tell your parents exactly what is going on and show them the messages, photos and videos that have been used to bully you.

Do tell them who is behind the bullying or who you suspect is involved.

Do recognise that what is being done to you is unacceptable and needs to be stopped.

Do report the abusive behaviour to the safety centres operated by Facebook and other social networking sites.

Do delete messages without reading them unless you are gathering evidence against the bully.

Do block cyber-bullies by every means possible. This can include blocking them on social networking sites and excluding them from instant messaging friend lists.

Don't ignore the cyber-bullying and hope that it will go away. It won't.

Don't say things online that you would not say face to face.

Don't try and retaliate. You could end up in trouble and be made to look like the perpetrator and not the victim.

Don't fight your parents. They are not the enemy. While they may not understand exactly what you are going through, they love you and have extremely protective instincts towards you.

Dos and Don'ts for Parents

The most important thing parents can do is support their child. They need the security of your love at this time. Questions can come later.

Do tell you child that you love them, support them, that they don't deserve this, and that you won't rest until something is done to put matters right.

Do take the matter seriously and approach the school, police or other authorities to help you deal with the problem.

Do persist until you get help and the problem is sorted out.

Do listen if your child wants to talk – and comfort them when their pain overwhelms them.

Do make an effort to understand how social networking sites and chat rooms operate. Ensure your teen has their profiles set as private and discourage the use of sites that may cause further cyber-bullying problems.

Do sign up to Facebook and similar sites and become friends with your child – especially if they are young. This gives you some access to what is going on. It is best to monitor things quietly and never be invasive or do something to embarrass your child.

Do be willing to allow your child to attend a different school if this is what they want.

Do direct your anger towards the cyber-bully and not your child – and then use it in a constructive manner to bring the abuse to an end.

Don't explode and shout at your child. They need your love and understanding more than anything else at this time.

Don't confiscate their cell phones, tablets, laptops and other devices. The fear of this happening is what stops many teens from confiding in their parents.

Don't try and place the blame on your teenager. Their self esteem is at an all time low and they need your support and encouragement.

Don't trivialise what your child is going through. Cyber-bullying is a big deal and a devastating experience.

Don't smother your teen. They need space and freedom and will resent you breathing down their neck 24/7.

Don't ignore signs that your teen is depressed or suicidal. Seek immediate help from a health professional.

Chapter Eight

How to Put an End to Cyber-Bullying

People who fight fire with fire usually end up with ashes.

Abigail Van Buren

Michelle was 16 when a group of girls at school turned against her. She had put on a bit of weight and her skin broke out meaning she no longer met the unwritten code for the group. The girls would message her inviting her to a party and when she arrived they would laugh and say it had just finished. Other tactics included texting her in the early hours of the morning and calling her names such as fatty, spot and loser. Michelle started eating even more as a comfort mechanism and the weight piled on. She spent hours locked in her room, reading texts and emails sent by these girls and crying. Her parents had no clue what was causing their daughter's pain until a friend of Michelle's told them. Her mother checked Michelle's email which she left open while showering and was shocked at the venom and hatred directed at her daughter. The family eventually moved to another city where Michelle was treated for her skin problems and a dietician helped her get her weight down. Michelle still suffers from depression and is angry she had to change her physical appearance and move to another town in order to find acceptance.

Cyber-bullying is never alright and you need to reach a place where you draw a metaphorical line in the sand and say 'no more.' Once you have made a decision to end the abuse, there are a number of options open to you. An important point to remember is that is best to ignore the bully but not the bullying. There are ways to find help and most bullies will continue their abusive actions until confronted with a force that is stronger than they are.

Questions to Consider

Identifying the enemy is an important part of ending the cyber-abuse. Here are some questions that will help you analyse what you are facing:

- do I know who the bully is
- were they a friend or acquaintance in the past or are they completely unknown to me
- are they a physical threat
- how frequently do they communicate
- what is their favoured means of communication
- do they use more than one medium of communication
- is there a particular thing they are attacking me over

Immediate Actions to Take

It is important to limit the bully's access as much as possible. Depending on their favoured form of communication, the following actions can be a step towards freedom:

- Change email addresses and ask trusted friends to keep your new one private.
- Change your cell phone number and only give the new one to close family and friends.
- Outlook Express and other email programs give you the option of blocking incoming emails. Block any email addresses the cyber-bully has used to contact you in the past.
- Contact moderators of chat rooms where the bully has harassed you and ask them to block the bully from accessing the site.
- Contact your internet service provider (ISP) and ask them to block the offender's email address and help you track down where the bullying messages originate from.
- If the cyber-bully is on Facebook or other social networking sites, block them permanently from being your friend.

Capture Evidence of Cyber-Bullying

Many cyber-bullies are internet savvy and wipe out their trail as they go. They do this by posting comments, and then delete them once their victim has read them and reacted. This means that their communication is no longer visible if the victim goes back to the site to show someone in authority. Others may use cheap pay-as-you-go cell phones that cannot be traced back to them.

It is important to capture evidence of cyber-bullying as a record of the abuse can be invaluable if the matter goes to the police or other authorities. There are a number of ways of doing this.

- Save all cell phone messages and photos that are abusive. If your phone has limited memory, download the evidence onto your computer or take photos of the messages and pictures on the screen. Store these in a safe place – preferably as a computer file and a printed copy.
- Save abusive emails into a separate folder or print them out and file them in date order.
- When a cyber-bullying comment is made in a chat room or on Facebook or similar, take a screenshot of it and save it. This is a simple process and is done in the following way:

1. Press the 'PrtScn' or 'Print Screen' button on your keyboard. This literally takes a picture of what is on your screen at the time.
2. Open Paint and click on 'paste'. This will open the screenshot as a picture in Paint.
3. Save and date the picture and place it into a folder created especially to collect your evidence. You could call the folder something like 'Cyber-Bully' or 'Cyber Evidence'.

It is a good idea to keep two cyber-bullying folders on your computer - one for documents and emails, and one for pictures and screenshots.

Handling Communication from Cyber-Bullies
There are three types of response to cyber-bullying: aggressive, passive and assertive. Many victims react aggressively or passively with little success. Here are some thoughts on what each of these methods look like:

Aggressive responses – in this case, the victim matches the bully by retaliating with abusive messages of their own. You may insult the bully through online messages, emails and texts in the hopes of deterring them. Unfortunately, this response normally inflames the situation. Another common response is to try and explain your actions, thoughts or beliefs to the cyber-bully. This is generally a waste of time as the bully is into control. They are convinced that they are right and won't listen to reason.

Passive responses – some people try and make themselves invisible to the cyber-bully or they may comply with their demands in order to keep the peace. This is not healthy and your tormentor will never be satisfied. Never adjust your behaviour to keep the peace unless you are obviously in the wrong.

Assertive responses – this is the best way to handle a cyber-bully. It may involve ignoring the bully while going over their head to site moderators and people in authority. It also includes actions whereby access is denied by changing email addresses and cell phone numbers. In effect it is saying, "I'm in charge here. Your behaviour is unacceptable and I'm not going to allow it".

From the outset, it is best to avoid any direct communication with the cyber-bully. They thrive on negative interactions and silence is extremely frustrating for them. Having said that, there are situations where a face-to-face meeting with the bully can be helpful. This should always be a mediated discussion with someone who has a measure of official authority and is familiar with what has been communicated electronically.

Educate Yourself about Cyber-Bullying
Knowledge is power. Read books, watch movies and research cyber-bullying in every way possible. When you recognise and understand what is happening, it is easier to take steps to put an end to it.

Set up coping strategies
Cyber-bullying is not something that should be handled alone. Find someone to confide in. This can be a parent, sibling, friend, teacher, pastor, counsellor or anyone that you trust. Show them the evidence you have collected and tell them how you feel. If the first person you speak to is afraid to be involved, try someone else. Keep asking for help until you find it.

Acknowledge your Pain
It's important to acknowledge the feelings that the cyber-bully evokes in you. You may be alarmed at the level of anger and rage, hurt and hate, but you need to face these feelings. If your stomach twists every time you see the bully's email address, or you have nightmares about them, you need to talk it through. A trained counsellor can be helpful in this type of situation.

Through all of the above, there is a core message that needs to be communicated to the person cyber-bullying you: *What you are doing is not acceptable or right. I am no longer going to be your victim and I will take this as far as I need to, to stop you.*

The period of confrontation and taking back power can be extremely difficult and emotional. In many cases the cyber-bully will intensify their attack for a time. It is all part of the process and will pass. Lean on supportive family and friends to get you through each day – and remember - it's alright to be bewildered, it's alright to be shocked, hurt and angry. It's alright to cry and beat your pillow. But it's never alright to sit back and do nothing when you're being cyber-bullied.

Chapter Nine

The Law and Cyber-Bullying

One would not expect a victim of rape to have to single-handedly identify, trace, catch, arrest, prosecute, convict and punish the person who raped her. Targets of bullying often find themselves doing all of these whilst those in positions of authority persistently abdicate and deny responsibility.

Tim Fields

Seth was in his first year at university and found himself the target of a cyber-bully. He wasn't sure who it was but soon determined not to let this person beat him. He realised that responding to the abusive messages was pointless and only led to an increase in the attack. Instead he reported the matter to the university, police and his local MP. He then located a bright young man in the IT department at college and asked for his help in tracking the origin of the emails and messages he was being bombarded with. With the cooperation of his internet service provider, they soon had the ID of the cyber-bully. It turned out to be a third-year, female student who was a loner and awkward around men. She had tried to strike up a conversation with Seth in the cafeteria one day and he unwittingly brushed her off. Hurt and angry, she made it her mission to get revenge by harassing him. She apologised, agreed to go for counselling and said she would not go near Seth in the future. Through Seth's efforts, the university, his MP and his friends all came to a deeper understanding of what cyber-bullying is and how painful it can be.

It is only in recent years that cyber-bullying has become a large problem and in many respects, the law is lagging behind. This does not mean that there is no way to stop cyber-bullying through legal channels. Although there may not be specific laws against cyber-abuse in your country, there are usually ways that serious offenders can be held accountable for their actions.

The daily Mail in the UK carried the following report on the 21st August 2009:

A teenager who posted a death threat on Facebook, yesterday became the first person in Britain to be jailed for bullying on a social networking site.

Keeley Houghton, 18, said she would kill Emily Moore, whom she had bullied for four years since they were at school together.

Houghton was sentenced to three months in a young offenders' institution and was also issued with a restraining order. This banned her from any contact with Emily, whether it be in person, via the internet or in any other manner for five years.

There have been several other cases around the world where cyber-bullies have been brought to account and even served jail time for their behaviour. This is an encouraging sign that the authorities and governments are starting to take cyber-bullying seriously.

If you are being persistently cyber-bullied and the content of the messages and communication is malicious, threatening and distressing, it is worth reporting it to the police. Depending on the type and frequency of the cyber-bullying, it may fit into one or more of the following categories:

Defamation is the act of spreading false information about a person. The consequences of defamation can include the ruining of your reputation, causing people to avoid you, and harm to your school, work or professional life. Defamation consists of libel and slander.

Libel is defined as the publication of untruths in writing, print, signs, or pictures that damage your reputation and lead to a loss of respect.

Slander is the action or crime of making false spoken statements that are damaging to your reputation. This is less common in cyber-bullying than libel or defamation but can include spoken abuse in video clips.

When making an accusation of libel or slander, you need to be able to produce evidence showing that:

- defamatory messages were conveyed
- these messages were published - meaning other people had access to them

- the accused must be identifiable as the sender and origin of these messages
- you must have suffered some harm to your reputation as a result of the communication

Harassment is the act of systematic, persistent, unwanted and annoying behaviours of a person or a group, that often include threats and demands.

Cyber-Bullying Laws
This is a topic that is changing and developing all the time. With this is mind, here is a look at cyber-bullying laws in some parts of the world. This is purely for interest and should not be taken as legal advice or acted on in any way.

Laws in Australia
The Australian included the following in an article about a website the government has introduced to help handle the problem of cyber-bullying. The news report was dated the 13th January 2012:

Legislation providing jail terms of up to 10 years for cyber-bullying has been in place in Victoria since June last year, with a charge of stalking applicable if the bullying is part of a pattern of conduct likely to cause physical or mental harm, or fear of it.

Laws in India
Haltabuse.org state that the Indian Information technology Act 2008 (amended) deals with the

problem of cyber-abuse more as an "intrusion on to the privacy of individual" than as regular cyber offences which are discussed in the IT Act 2008. As a result the most used provision for regulating cyber stalking in India is section 72 of the Indian information technology act (Amended), 2008 which runs as follows;

Section 72: Breach of confidentiality and privacy:
Save as otherwise provided in this Act or any other law for the time being in force, any person who, in pursuant of any of the powers conferred under this Act, rules or regulations made there under, has secured access to any electronic record, book, register, correspondence, information, document or other material without the consent of the person concerned discloses such electronic record, book, register, correspondence, information, document or other material to any other person shall be punished with imprisonment for a term which may extend to two years, or with fine which may extend to one lakh rupees, or with both.

Laws in New Zealand
The New Zealand Herald carried an article on cyber-bullying and the law on January 22nd 2012. This discussed how victims may one day be able to access an *'internet enforcer capable of imposing fines, ordering apologies or even terminating the offender's internet account.'*

The article went on to say, *'Laws would make it a criminal offence to encourage someone to commit suicide, to post "intimate images" online without the subject's consent and to "maliciously impersonate" someone on social media such as Facebook and Twitter.'*

Cyberbullying.org.nz gave information on laws existing in New Zealand as of January 2012:

Cyber-bullying can be a criminal offence under a range of different laws, including sections 249-252 of the Crimes Act. The age of criminal responsibility in New Zealand is 10 years. If young people commit an offence they may face warnings, police diversions, or a Family Group Conference. Young people over 16 who commit an offence are treated as adults by the courts.

Education Law in New Zealand (Education Act 1998) includes the National Administrative Guideline 5, which says that schools are to provide a "safe physical and emotional environment for students". This includes addressing behaviours (such as cyber-bullying) that occur outside school but which have implications for student's well-being while at school.

Laws in South Africa
Lawlibrary.co.za provided the following update from the KwaZulu-Natal Law Society on the 4th March 2011:

Using cyberspace to taunt, slander, intimidate or harass a person online will soon be illegal under the new Protection from Harassment Bill, which will make "cyber-bullying" punishable under the law and could even land the bully behind bars.

Laws in the UK

Digizen.org outlines the laws in the UK that can be applied to cyber-bullying. Although it is not regarded as a criminal offence at present, there are criminal laws that can be applied. These include:

The Protection from Harassment Act 1997which has both criminal and civil provision, the Malicious Communications Act 1988, section 127 of the Communications Act 2003 and the Public Order Act 1986.The age of criminal responsibility in the UK starts at 10.

Laws in the USA

Various states in the USA have introduced cyber-bullying laws while others are still working on them. Pressconnects.com reported the following on the 21st January 2012:

Legislation was introduced in Albany on Jan. 9 this year aimed at cracking down on cyber-bullying. Sen. Jeff Klein, D-Bronx, said the bill would update the state's stalking and harassment laws to cover electronic bullying and allow for criminal charges in cyber-bullying incidents under the state's hate crime statutes.

Cyberbullying.us displayed a table dated January 2012 that gave figures about which states had bullying laws in place and which were considering updating them and making provision for areas such as electronic harassment. A brief summary of facts revealed the following:

- 48 states had bullying laws
- 11 states were considering updating the law
- 14 states proposed including cyber-bullying
- 38 states were looking at including electronic harassment
- 48 states were considering school policy

It is inevitable that in years to come, cyber-bullying laws will continue to be introduced and will be updated as technology advances. In the meantime, you can help the process by writing to relevant people in government and law enforcement and ask for the issues involved with cyber-bullying to be specifically addressed by the laws of your country.

Chapter Ten

Long Term Healing from Cyber-Bullying

Every adversity, every failure, and every heartache, carries with it the seed of an equivalent or greater benefit.

Napoleon Hill

Penny was in her 50's when she first ventured into the online world. A spinster, she was lonely and soon found a number of chat rooms where she made some online friends. One of these was a man who went by the name of Nathan21. His photo showed a handsome blonde man in his early 50's. Nathan21 was charming and witty and soon she was chatting to him every night after work. All went well until he started asking personal questions about her finances and sexuality. She withdrew but he knew enough about her that he called her at work. She asked him to leave her alone but he became more and more persistent. He wanted to know where she was at weekends and who she was seeing. One night he sent her a video clip. He had tracked her down and followed her home, filming her while she had no idea what was going on. This terrified her and she emailed the chat room administrator informing them of what was going on. Nathan21 was blocked permanently but soon reappeared as Malcolm99. Penny sought legal advice and Malcolm99 finally backed off after a lawyer's letter was emailed to him. Penny still looks over her shoulder and lives in fear that he might surprise her one day. She has moved house and changed all her contact details in an effort to hide herself from this man.

Cyber-bullying can be cruel, vindictive and frightening. Even when it comes to an end, the emotional and social effects can linger indefinitely if not actively addressed. This applies not only to you, but also to your family members and loved ones. Here are some thoughts and suggestions on how you can find healing in this type of situation.

Forgive the Cyber-Bully
Strange as it may sound, it is important to forgive your cyber-bully. Even though they have caused you immense pain and interfered with school or work life, friendships, and may have forced you to change your lifestyle and habits, you need to forgive them. If you don't, angry thoughts of revenge and hatred will consume you and divert your focus away from what is good in life. Bitterness is a poison that will slowly destroy relationships and rob you of hope and joy. Don't allow a cyber-bully's abuse to linger and ruin your life.

Be Accountable to Someone you Trust
Once the cyber-bullying comes to an end, you may feel a great sense of relief and freedom ... but you may also be surprised by the doubts that pop up. *Maybe I overreacted. She's not such a bad person really. Maybe I really do have a problem with the way I chat online/write/communicate.* It helps to have a trusted friend or counsellor on hand who knows what you've been through. A quick chat with them

will help you get your perspective back and lift your spirits. Depending on the level of cyber-abuse, it can take months or even years for your emotions to fully recover from the attack.

Beware of Danger Spots
As far as possible, don't frequent sites and chat rooms where the abuse was perpetrated unless you know you are safe. For sites such as Facebook, it is possible to block a person and keep your profile private so they have no access to you at all. Don't post personal details anywhere on the internet at any time. Protect your online work by changing passwords from time to time and use strong ones that cannot be easily hacked. Those with a combination of numbers and letters are best.

Learn about Cyber-Bullying
Read books, surf the net and talk to people who have experienced similar problems with cyber-bullying. It helps to understand the problem and is encouraging to read about other peoples' pain and how they triumphed at the end of the day.

Help Others in Similar Situations
Once you have healed enough, be willing to help others who are going through a similar experience. Just talking to someone who understands them can be helpful and it can be a positive experience for you as well. This can be an informal process as you interact with people or you may want to join an anti-bullying group that can provide you with specific opportunities to tell your story.

Volunteer to Speak to Schools
Teens are vulnerable to cyber-abuse as much of their social interaction is done through texting and online communication. Many of them will not recognise harassment over the internet as bullying and hearing someone share their story can open their eyes to what is happening to them.

Surround Yourself with Positive Messages
After experiencing a prolonged bout of cyber-bullying, it is inevitable that the accusations and feelings will creep back from time to time. Write out a list of what you like about yourself and read it through when you feel vulnerable. Another good idea is to hang a picture or poster in your home that signifies your victory. This can be a figure holding a trophy above their head or a runner bursting through the finishing line. What you fill your mind with is extremely important and will give you the power to overcome the darkest thoughts on the longest days. Look at how far you've come and determine to keep pressing on.

Seek Ongoing Counselling and Prayer
The effects and pain of cyber-bullying tend to resurface every so often. Memories may be triggered by reading a newspaper article, watching a movie or seeing someone related to the cyber-bully. If you hit a bad patch and feel down and alone, go for another counselling session or call on someone who supported you while you dealt with the cyber-bully. Prayer from a minister or pastor can be healing as well as instrumental in helping you regain your focus.

Don't feel condemned if you are still dealing with the pain months or even years after the cyber-bullying has stopped. Your self-worth has been dealt a harsh blow and it can take an extended period of time to learn to trust people again and not feel fearful when engaging others on social networks and similar. The most important thing to do is keep moving forward and always remember that Cyber-bullying is never, never, never alright!

Chapter One References:

http://www.abc.net.au/news/2009-05-07/elite-schools-horrific-cyber-bullying-case/1675916

http://www.dailymail.co.uk/femail/article-1236481/Bullied-bedrooms-Vicious-cyber-bullying-driving-young-girls-deaths.html

http://abcnews.go.com/Health/cyber-bullying-factor-suicide-massachusetts-teen-irish-immigrant/story?id=9660938

http://www.stuff.co.nz/national/education/3305306/Vicious-Facebook-attack-on-new-Burnside-High-principal

http://abcnews.go.com/US/victim-secret-dorm-sex-tape-commits-suicide/story?id=11758716

http://www.dailymail.co.uk/news/article-1347034/Facebook-cyberbullying-Schoolgirls-arrested-creating-fake-page-naked-pictures.html

http://www.dailymail.co.uk/news/article-1363723/Bullies-pose-teenagers-boyfriend-Facebook-tell-hes-committed-suicide.html

http://www.stuff.co.nz/the-press/news/6036349/Gossip-forces-girl-to-move-after-sex-video

http://www.dailymail.co.uk/tvshowbiz/article-2078635/Military-Wives-Choir-Samantha-Stevenson-taunted-Facebook-Twitter-tattoos.html

71

Chapter Nine References

http://www.dailymail.co.uk/news/article-1208147/First-cyberbully-jailed-Facebook-death-threats.html#ixzz1k4k3381U

http://www.theaustralian.com.au/news/nation/government-launches-cyber-bullying-website/story-e6frg6nf-1226243273609

http://www.haltabuse.org/resources/laws/india.shtml

http://www.nzherald.co.nz/nz/news/article.cfm?c_id=1&objectid=10772670

http://www.cyberbullying.org.nz/teachers/

http://www.lawlibrary.co.za/notice/updates/2011/issue_05/govtandleg_legislation.htm

http://www.digizen.org/downloads/CYBERBULLYING.pdf

http://www.pressconnects.com/article/20120121/NEWS01/201210347/Stopping-bully-Schools-ramping-up-education-staff

http://www.cyberbullying.us/Bullying_and_Cyberbullying_Laws.pdf

Useful Resources

www.digizen.org

www.cyberbullying.org

www.cyberbullying.org.nz

www.lifeafteradultbullying.com

www.bullyonline.org

www.ncpc.org/cyberbullying

About the Author

Debbie Roome was born and raised in Zimbabwe and later spent fifteen years in South Africa. In 2006 she moved to New Zealand with her husband and five children. Writing has been her passion since the age of six and she loves to write stories that touch people's lives and turn them towards God. Her major writing achievements include the trophy for Runner-up to the Writer of the Year, South Africa,2004; placing second out of 7000 in the FaithWriters.com "Best of the Best" contest for 2007; and receiving the trophy from the South African Writers' Circle for the best self-published book of 2007. Her novel, *Embracing Change,* won First Place in the Rose & Crown New Novels Competition of 2009. She entered the first chapter of Magnitude 7.1 & 6.3 in the Faithwriter's "Page Turner" Competition in 2010 and was awarded second place. Debbie's writing has also opened doors for public speaking and she is often asked to share her life story and her experiences as a writer.

www.debbieroome.com
debbieroome@gmail.com

Books by Debbie Roome

A collection of stories about the Canterbury earthquakes. More than 40 men, women and children share experiences that will shock, amaze and inspire. Includes black and white photos and a firsthand account of the 1929 Murchison earthquake.

Inspirational romance that took first place in the 2009 Rose & Crown novel-writing competition in the UK. This heart-warming story is set in New Zealand and South Africa and has a strong theme of hope and forgiveness.

Lindsay's life in Christchurch is turned upside down when Mind Games and evidence drag her into a murder case – as a suspect. This book contains three interrelated cosy mysteries that are centred round board games.

Moods of Africa is a collection of inspirational short stories set in various parts of Africa. These stories have a Christian theme and are sure to tug on your heart strings. Kindle version only.

Tender Christmas Tales is a collection of short Christmas stories with a Christian theme. Read about the dying girl who held the hands of two fathers and the unborn baby who received his first Christmas gift from his mother. Kindle version only.

www.ingramcontent.com/pod-product-compliance
Lightning Source LLC
Chambersburg PA
CBHW060159290526
45789CB00003B/1085